Sugar Inspirations

Anniversary Cakes

MARY TIPTON

Published 1995 by Merehurst Limited
Ferry House, 51–57 Lacy Road, Putney,
London SW15 1PR

Copyright © Merehurst Limited 1995
ISBN 1-85391-457-6

A catalogue record for this book is available from the
British Library.

Editor: Helen Southall
Design: Rita Wüthrich
Photography by Ken Field and Alan Marsh

Typeset by Servis Filmsetting Ltd, Manchester
Colour separation by P & W Graphics Pty Ltd, Singapore
Printed in Italy by Milanostampa SpA

Contents

Introduction   4

Anniversary Cakes

First (Cotton)   6

Seventh (Copper)   10

Tenth (Tin)   14

Thirteenth (Lace)   18

Twentieth (China)   22

Twenty-fifth (Silver)   26

Thirtieth (Pearl)   30

Fortieth (Ruby)   34

Fiftieth (Gold)   38

Basic Recipes   41

Templates   44

Acknowledgements   48

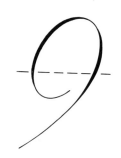

Introduction

This book brings together ideas for anniversary cakes for both the early and later years with designs suitable for intimate, romantic occasions as well as more formal parties and presentations.

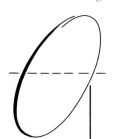

Tradition (and commerce) dictates the association of particular types of gift with specific wedding anniversaries, as seen in the table on page 5. As far as possible, these themes are reflected in the cakes presented in this book. However, many of the designs are interchangeable – a different colour or inscription is often all that is required. It will be evident from the table that European and American anniversary themes often differ but, generally, a suitable colour scheme can be found.

One of the most satisfying aspects of cake decorating is to put one's own stamp on a design, and it is hoped that the ideas in this book will serve as inspiration for your own creativity.

Equipment
In addition to the basic cake decorating equipment of palette knives,

scrapers, piping bags and tubes, smoothers, crimpers, paper and pencil, the designs in this book use some other equipment, most of which can be found in sugarcraft or cake-decorating shops. More conventional items include a Garrett frill cutter (although a round fluted biscuit cutter, together with a smaller plain round cutter for the centre, will do) and daisy, petunia and leaf cutters. Three basic modelling tools are required:
Ball tool This has a different-sized ball shape at each end. It is used for indenting hollow shapes and for smoothing cut edges, such as the edges of round petals.
Shell tool This is shell-shaped at one end and has a plastic blade at the other.
Veiner tool This is shaped to a different-sized, flattened, curved point

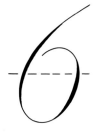

at each end. It is used for subtle indentations and smoothing joins.

For some of the designs in this book, conventional equipment is put to an alternative use, for example plain piping tubes are sometimes used as cutters, and for the First Anniversary Cake a set of plastic dowels (usually used inside hollow pillars to support tiered cakes) is used to form the folds in sugarpaste swags (see page 8).

However, not all the equipment used can be bought in a cake-decorating shop; sometimes you need to look elsewhere. For example, for creating a tailor-made embosser, a perspex photo frame is perfect (see page 14)! For the Ruby Wedding Cake (see page 34), a shaped side scraper is required. If you haven't got one, you can improvise by cutting a hole with a hole puncher in a plain side scraper.

Traditional wedding themes (right) are a wonderful source of inspiration for creative cake designs. By adapting some of the ideas in this book and using different colours and numerals (such as those on this page and on pages 46–47), you can create a cake for any anniversary.

	European	American
1st	Cotton	Gold jewellery
2nd	Paper	Garnet
3rd	Leather	Pearls
4th	Fruit and flowers	Blue topaz
5th	Wood	Sapphire
6th	Sugar	Amethyst
7th	Wool or copper	Onyx
8th	Bronze or Pottery	Tourmaline
9th	Pottery or Willow	Lapis lazuli
10th	Tin	Diamond jewellery
12th	Silk or Linen	Jade
13th	Lace	Citrine
14th	Ivory	Opal
15th	Crystal	Ruby
20th	China	Emerald
25th	Silver	Silver
30th	Pearl	Pearl
35th	Coral	Emerald
40th	Ruby	Ruby
45th	Sapphire	Sapphire
50th	Gold	Gold
60th	Diamond	Diamond
70th	Platinum	—

First Anniversary Cake

Theme: Cotton

Two modelled teddy bears appear to have helped in draping the 'cotton' swags

around this appealing cake.

Materials

20cm (8 inch) round cake
Apricot glaze
1kg (2lb) white almond paste
Clear alcohol (such as vodka) for brushing
875g (1¾lb) ivory sugarpaste
125g (4oz) ivory royal icing
Food colourings
125g (4oz) modelling paste (see page 41)
Cornflour for dusting

Equipment

28cm (11 inch) round cake board
1cm (⅜ inch) plain piping tube
Pieces of foam
Ball modelling tool
Fine paintbrush
Plain piping tubes (nos. 1, 2 and 3)
Stencil paper or till roll
Masking tape
Scriber
Small paper piping bag
Set of plastic dowels
Veiner tool

Preparing the cake

1 Brush the cake with apricot glaze and cover with 875g (1¾lb) almond paste, reserving the trimmings. Brush with alcohol and cover with the ivory sugarpaste.

2 Centre the cake on the cake board and cover the board around the base of the cake with about half of the ivory royal icing. Leave to dry overnight.

Modelling the teddy bears

3 Colour the remaining 125g (4oz) almond paste golden brown and form it into a roll of 2.5cm (1 inch) diameter. Cut a 2.5cm (1 inch) length for each body and another piece one-third this size for each head.

4 Form each body into a teardrop shape and place it, wide end down, on a non-stick surface. Form the heads into balls and flatten them slightly at the front.

5 To make the legs, shape the remaining coloured almond paste into a roll of 1cm (½ inch) diameter, and cut four 2.5cm (1 inch) lengths. Push one end of each piece up to form the feet. Round the other ends and flatten on one side. Gently press the legs to either side of each body shape.

6 Roll out a little uncoloured almond paste thinly (see Tip on page 8) and make the pads for the feet by cutting two circles with the tip of a plain piping tube. Press the pads into place on the soles of the feet.

7 The arms are modelled in a similar fashion from four 2.5cm (1 inch) lengths of almond paste cut from a 5mm (¼ inch) diameter roll. Attach these to the upper bodies, pressing gently. Support the out-stretched arms with pieces of foam until they have dried.

8 Cut four 5mm (¼ inch) pieces from the same 5mm (¼ inch) roll to form the ears. Roll each of these into a ball, flatten slightly, then press a 5mm (¼ inch) circle of uncoloured paste on to each. Position the ears on each side of each head. Fix and shape by pressing with a ball tool.

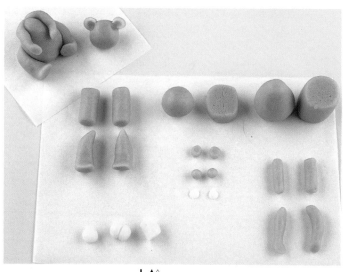

scallop shape, cutting through the layers of paper. Fix the paper template around the cake, securing with masking tape, and scribe scallops on to the side of the cake.

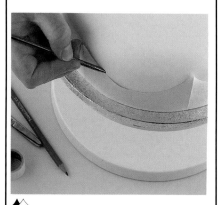

Tip

For a clean finish when rolling almond paste or sugarpaste thinly, as required for the pads on the teddy bears' feet and paws, and for the eyes, roll out the paste between two sheets of firm plastic. Icing sugar is not required.

9 For the muzzles, shape a little uncoloured almond paste into a 1cm (½ inch) diameter roll. Cut off a 1cm (½ inch) length and form into a ball. Carefully cut this in half and apply one piece to the front of each head.

10 The features can be painted on using a fine paintbrush, or a food colouring pen. Alternatively, the eyes and noses can be cut from thinly rolled (see Tip) black sugarpaste, using a plain no. 2 piping tube as a cutter. Press these features into place, then paint in the mouths.

Making swags and bows

11 Cut a strip of stencil paper or till roll (or greaseproof or non-stick paper) that is as wide as the depth of the cake, and long enough to fit around it. Fold this into six equal sections and cut one long side to a

12 Pipe a small bulb border at the base of the cake using ivory royal icing in a paper piping bag fitted with a plain no. 3 tube.

13 Colour the modelling paste as desired and roll it out thinly on a work surface lightly dusted with cornflour. Cut six rectangles, each measuring 13x8cm (5x3¼ inches). Cover the rectangles with plastic wrap to prevent them drying out. Brush along one marked scallop line on the cake side with cooled boiled water.

14 Place one rectangle of modelling paste over a set of plastic dowels and ease the paste into the gaps between the dowels to create folds. Using both hands, gather the ends between your fingers and thumbs, and press the folds together as you lift the paste away from the dowels.

15 Position the swag on the cake side, pressing the ends in place and pinching away any excess. With a veiner tool, arrange the folds and gently press them against the cake

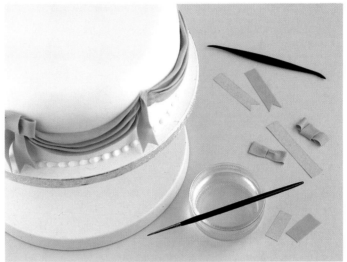

side. Repeat, positioning swags all around the cake.

16 Roll the remaining paste thinly and cut it into strips 1.5cm (⅝ inch) wide. From these strips cut 12 ribbon tails slightly shorter than the distance between the cake board and the top of the swags. Cut six 8cm (3¼ inch) lengths to form the loops and six 3cm (1¼ inch) lengths to form the knots. Reserve the trimmings.

17 Moisten the joins in the swags with a damp paintbrush and press two ribbon tails to each join. The tails can be twisted slightly to add movement. Moisten the ends of the loop pieces and fold into the centre. Moisten the ends of the knot pieces. Place a loop section centrally across each knot piece, then fold over the ends of the knot pieces, pressing gently to secure. Moisten the back of

each knot and press each bow in place to disguise the ends of the swags and tails.

Finishing

18 Trace the inscription on page 46 on to greaseproof or non-stick paper. Lay the paper on top of the cake and use a scriber to scribe the outline on to the surface.

19 Colour the remaining royal icing to match the swags, and transfer to a paper piping bag fitted with a no. 1 tube. Use to pipe the inscription.

20 Fix the teddy bears in place using a little royal icing. Roll out a little of the remaining modelling paste and cut a length for the teddy bears to hold. Trim the board edge with ribbon or a paper band.

Tip

A more commercial finish can be achieved by using plastic moulds which are available for swags and bows.

Seventh Anniversary Cake

Theme: Copper

Piped copper=coloured chrysanthemums adorn this elegant royal=iced cake

that is stunningly edged with a runout collar.

Materials
18cm (7 inch) hexagonal cake
Apricot glaze
750g (1½lb) almond paste
750g (1½lb) royal icing
Copper and green food colourings

Equipment
28cm (11 inch) hexagonal cake board
Scriber
Masking tape
Waxed paper or cellophane
Small and medium-sized piping bags
Plain piping tubes (nos. 1, 2 and 3)
Paintbrush
Craft knife or scalpel
Angle-poise or desk lamp
Palette knife
Ribbon piping tubes (nos. 31R and 32R)
Flower nail

Preparing the cake

1 Brush the cake with apricot glaze and cover with the almond paste. Cover the top and each side separately so that all the edges are sharp. Leave until firm, then place the cake on the cake board.

2 Flat ice the cake with royal icing tinted pale copper, coating the top and sides separately to give square edges to the cake top. Leave to dry for 24 hours, then apply a second coat. Dry again, then apply a third coat. When the final coat is complete, coat the board around the base of the cake. Dry for 24 hours.

Making the runouts

3 To make the base collar, cut a piece of greaseproof or non-stick paper the size of the cake board and fold it in half. Unfold it and trace the outline for the runout collar on page 45 on to one side. Refold the paper with the tracing on top and cut along the inner outline 5mm (¼ inch) **outside** the traced line. Slip the outer part of the template over the cake, aligning the pattern with the cake sides. Scribe the scalloped shape on to the coated board.

4 Trace the outlines for the runout collar and numeral on page 45 on to greaseproof or non-stick paper and re-trace on to a thicker piece of paper. Fix to a flat surface with masking tape.

5 Secure a piece of waxed paper or cellophane over the collar outline with pieces of masking tape, ensuring that the paper is perfectly flat. Cut some pieces of waxed paper or cellophane a little larger than the numeral and fix one of these over the traced outline, securing with small dots of royal icing.

6 Colour about 250g (8oz) of freshly beaten royal icing a deeper tint of copper than the cake coating. Adjust the consistency so that it is suitable for writing, and put a quantity into a small piping bag fitted with a no. 1 plain piping tube. Tint a similar amount deeper again and put it into another small piping bag fitted with a no. 1 tube. Thin the remaining royal icing to runout consistency (see page 41) and pour it into two medium-sized piping bags, each of them fitted with a plain no. 2 piping tube.

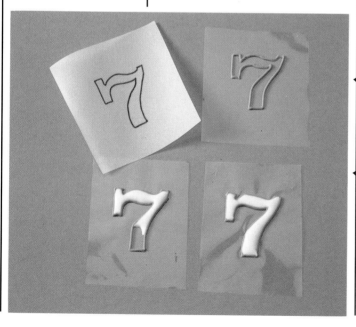

7 Pipe the inner and outer outlines of the collar using the no. 1 tube and paler icing. Flood in the runout icing in 5cm (2 inch) sections, using a paintbrush if necessary to tease the icing into the corners. Having completed one section, flood the section to its left, then flood the section to the right of the first.

8 Continue flooding the collar in this fashion, working on alternate areas on either side of the starter section. When the final section is flooded, there should be no visible join in the collar. Cut a cross in the centre of the waxed paper with a craft knife or scalpel; this will help to release tension as the icing dries, and prevent the collar from cracking. As soon as it is finished, place the runout under a warm lamp to dry.

9 Using a similar technique, outline the numeral using the no. 1 tube and deeper copper-coloured icing. Flood the shape using the runout icing, then carefully slide a palette knife under the waxed paper to free it from the drawing underneath. Slide the runout on to a flat surface and place it under the lamp to dry. Repeat the process with the remaining numerals, making a total of four plus some extras in case of breakages.

10 To make the base collar, pipe over the scribed outline on the cake board using a no. 1 tube, then flood a section at a time, as for the top collar. Use a paintbrush to tease the icing into the join at the base of the cake. Dry this runout as quickly as possible before the runout icing has time to dissolve the coating underneath. Put the cake under the lamp and turn it every 10 minutes or so to dry every section of the collar.

11 When both top and base collars are dry, decorate the edges with dots of royal icing coloured a deep copper, using a no. 1 tube.

Making the flowers

12 Cut some 2.5cm (1 inch) squares of waxed paper (you will need one for each flower, and some spares). Fill a piping bag fitted with a ribbon tube with well-beaten, full-peak royal icing coloured a deep shade of copper. (To achieve an interesting effect, colour two batches of icing in different shades of copper and put them both together in the same piping bag.)

13 Fix a square of waxed paper to a flower nail with a dot of royal icing and pipe a bulb of white royal icing in the centre with a plain no. 3 piping tube.

14 Pipe the petals using the copper icing and ribbon tube. Start near the top of the bulb and pipe a circle of petals to meet in and cover the centre. For the short petal effect, squeeze out the icing as you move the bag upwards, then stop squeezing and pull away sharply. Add a second row of petals below and in between those in the first row. Repeat with two additional rows, piping the petals to follow the curve of the centre bulb. Towards the base of the bulb, pipe the petals slightly longer and angled away from the bulb. The final row is piped flat on the waxed paper. Remove the paper from the nail and leave the flower to dry.

15 Repeat to make ten flowers in all, plus some spares. By varying the sizes of the white bulbs, and using large or small ribbon tubes (31R or 32R), you can produce flowers of different sizes.

Finishing

16 Pipe the bottom border of plain shells using a no. 3 tube and pale copper icing. Using a no. 1 tube, and pale copper icing, pipe a scalloped line down both sides of each corner around the cake. On alternate sides, fix a runout numeral with a few dots of royal icing. Pipe a short stem and leaf on the remaining sides, using a no. 3 tube and green royal icing. Fix a flower to each stem.

17 Pipe stems and leaves on the cake top using green royal icing. Fix an odd number of flowers (seven is an appropriate number) in a spray arrangement. Secure the numeral in place on top of the cake with dots of royal icing.

18 Remove the runout collar from the waxed paper. Using a no. 2 tube and pale copper royal icing, pipe a line on the top edge of the cake. Position the collar over this and carefully lower into place. Pipe pale copper linework inside the top edge of the collar using a no. 2 tube overpiped with a no. 1 tube. Pipe a line round the board just inside the edge using a no. 2 tube. Trim the board edge with ribbon or paper band.

Tenth Anniversary Cake

Theme: Tin

Tin is a white metal so this anniversary bell is decorated in pure white.

The embossing and the raised flowers are emphasized by the shadows they cast.

Materials

20cm (8 inch) diameter
bell-shaped cake
Apricot glaze
1.25kg (2½lb) almond
paste
250g (8oz) royal icing
Clear alcohol (such as
vodka) for brushing
1.25kg (2½lb) white
sugarpaste
125g (4oz) modelling
paste (see page 41)

Equipment

Piece of clear,
firm plastic
Paper piping bags
Plain piping tubes (nos.
1 and 2)
20cm (8 inch) and
25cm (10 inch) round
cake boards
2.5cm (1 inch) plain
crimper (optional)
Primrose cutter
Foam sponge (optional)
Ball modelling tool
Calyx cutter
Blossom plunger cutter
Non-toxic adhesive
3 loops and tails in
narrow white ribbon

Preparing the cake

1. Brush the cake with apricot glaze and cover the top and sides with the almond paste.

Making the embosser

2. Trace the appropriate motif on page 46 or 47 on to greaseproof or non-stick paper. Place the tracing face-down on a light-coloured surface and cover with a clear piece of firm plastic (e.g. a perspex photo frame).

3. Transfer a little royal icing to a piping bag fitted with a no. 2 piping tube, and pipe the motif on to the plastic, following the outline. Leave to dry.

Using the embosser

4. Brush the almond paste with alcohol and cover with sugarpaste, smoothing out any creases.

5. Gently but firmly press the embosser into the sugarpaste at the front of the cake. It may be necessary to rock the embosser from side to side so that even pressure is applied to the whole design.

6. Place the cake centrally on the 20cm (8 inch) cake board – it will overhang slightly. If desired, decorate the bottom edge of the cake with a plain crimper. Leave to dry.

10 The calyx cutter flowers are shaped by placing each flower face-up in the palm of your hand or on a piece of foam sponge, and stroking the ball tool from the tip to the centre of each petal to curve it.

11 To make the handle for the bell, cut a strip of modelling paste 1cm (½ inch) wide and 15–18cm (6–7 inches) long, lay it over a 6cm (2½ inch) diameter curve (such as a 400g/14oz food can), and leave it to dry for at least 24 hours.

Finishing
12 Place the 20cm (8 inch) cake board centrally on the larger board, securing with non-toxic adhesive. Coat the exposed board with royal icing.

13 Using a no. 2 piping tube and white royal icing, pipe a scalloped line around the base of the bell, then pipe a bell flower at the top of each scallop. Over-pipe the first scalloped line, using the same tube.

14 Fix the bell handle and ribbons in place with a little royal icing, then attach the flowers in a cascade down the side of the bell. Using a no. 1 tube and white royal icing, pipe centres into the flowers, and curving flower stems.

15 Using a no. 2 tube and white royal icing, decorate the cake board with a reverse 'S' and 'C' scroll border. Trim the board with ribbon or paper banding.

Variations
This is a versatile design which can be adapted for any anniversary simply by altering the embossed motif and the colour scheme, as can be seen from the cream and gold fiftieth anniversary cake illustrated.

Interesting effects can be achieved by making the flowers initially in pastel colours, then spraying them in deeper tints using an airbrush.

Flowers and bell handle
7 Make the flowers from white modelling paste rolled out as thinly as possible. You will need about 60 flowers in assorted sizes.

8 The flowers used on the cake illustrated were made using primrose and calyx cutters, with a few plunger-cutter blossoms. Keep the cut-out pieces of paste covered with plastic wrap while you work on one flower at a time.

9 To shape the primroses, place each cut-out flower face-down on the palm of your hand or on a piece of foam sponge. Using a ball modelling tool, stroke the tip of each petal from the edge towards the centre to cup it slightly. Turn the flower over and gently roll the ball tool in the centre. Leave to dry.

Tips

This bell shape may appear difficult to cut into portions. The easiest method is to cut it straight down through the centre, then place half, cut-side down, on a cutting board, and cut into slices and fingers in the usual way.

Ribbon loops and tails are very simple to make. Fold a length of ribbon into a figure-of-eight shape, leaving a length of 'tail' at each end. Twist a piece of 28-gauge wire round the centre. Use the wire to secure the ribbon to the cake. Loops and tails can be made in various sizes, with long or short tails.

Thirteenth Anniversary Cake

Theme: Lace

Deep scallops of delicate icing lace, cornelli piping and brush embroidery – derived from

Guipure lace – emphasize the lace theme of this romantic cake.

Materials

18cm (7 inch) heart cake
Apricot glaze
750g (1½lb) almond paste
Clear alcohol (such as vodka) for brushing
750g (1½lb) white sugarpaste
375g (12oz) royal icing
Lemon yellow and green food colourings
Piping gel

Equipment

30cm (12 inch) round cake board
Masking tape
Scriber
Waxed paper or cellophane
Piping bags
Plain piping tubes (nos. 1, 2 and 3)
Piece of foam sponge
No. 3 sable paintbrush

Preparing the cake

1 Brush the cake with apricot glaze and cover with the almond paste. Brush the almond paste with alcohol and cover with the white sugarpaste. Centre the cake on the cake board and coat the board around the base of the cake with about half the royal icing. Leave to dry.

2 Cut a strip of greaseproof or non-stick paper the length of one side of the cake and fold into four. Trace the side template outline on page 44 on to the top section of the folded strip, then cut round the outline to make a template. Tape the template to each side of the cake in turn and use the point of a scriber to mark the scallop pattern in the icing.

Where the scallops join, mark the positions for the layers of lace by scribing horizontal lines 1.5cm (¾ inch) apart.

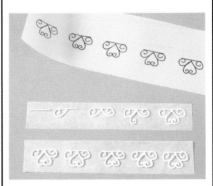

Making the lace

3 Using the pattern on page 44, trace a row of lace pieces on to greaseproof or non-stick paper. Cut strips of waxed paper or cellophane slightly wider than the height of the lace pattern and fix a strip over the pattern using dots of royal icing. Pipe the lace pieces in yellow or white royal icing, using a no. 1 tube. When the strip is complete, release the waxed paper from the tracing and slide it on to a flat surface to dry. You will need 40–50 individual pieces of lace, each in yellow and white.

Tips

The pattern for the brush embroidery may be embossed on to the cake top, instead of scribed. Make an embosser as described in the instructions for the Tenth Anniversary Cake on page 14, and use immediately the cake has been coated in sugarpaste.

Cornelli work is a continuous line of piping in a close pattern of curves, near to each other but not touching. The piping tube is held at an angle of 45° to the surface of the cake, with the tip touching, or very close to, the surface.

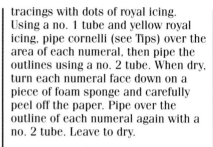

Making the numerals

4 Trace the numerals on page 44 on to greaseproof or non-stick paper, and re-trace on to thicker paper. Cut pieces of waxed paper or cellophane slightly larger than the numerals and fix them over the tracings with dots of royal icing. Using a no. 1 tube and yellow royal icing, pipe cornelli (see Tips) over the area of each numeral, then pipe the outlines using a no. 2 tube. When dry, turn each numeral face down on a piece of foam sponge and carefully peel off the paper. Pipe over the outline of each numeral again with a no. 2 tube. Leave to dry.

Brush embroidery

5 Trace the flower design on page 44 on to greaseproof or non-stick paper, place it carefully in position on top of the cake, and scribe the design on to the icing.

6 Put about 125g (4oz) royal icing in a bowl and beat in 1 teaspoon piping gel. This will prevent the icing from drying whilst you are working. Colour half the icing yellow and the remainder green and put each into a piping bag fitted with a no. 2 tube.

7 The technique of brush embroidery involves piping in the outline of each petal or leaf and brushing the soft icing inwards with a dampened brush, leaving a bold outline at the edge and a thin film of icing in the centre. First pipe in the stems, then begin to work on those parts of the design that appear to lie in the background, piping the outlines quite boldly. Dip a paintbrush in water, then squeeze the bristles to create a flat or chisel end to the brush. Brush the icing down from the outside to the centre using smooth, long strokes. Gradually work towards the foreground areas of the design. Pipe dots for the stamens.

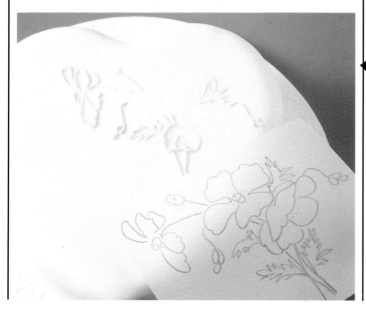

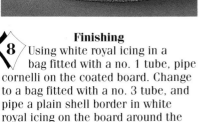

Finishing

8 Using white royal icing in a bag fitted with a no. 1 tube, pipe cornelli on the coated board. Change to a bag fitted with a no. 3 tube, and pipe a plain shell border in white royal icing on the board around the base of the cake.

9 The numerals are attached to the cake top using dots of royal icing. To fix the lace, pipe a line of icing with a no. 1 tube along the lowest horizontal line in one of the scallops. Secure pieces of yellow lace to this, ensuring they all lie at the same angle (about 45° to the cake). Do the same on the next and succeeding horizontal lines and in the remaining scallops around the cake until they are all fitted.

10 Fix pieces of white lace in the same way along the upper, scalloped line. Pipe tiny yellow dots above the white lace, using a no. 1 tube. Trim the board edge with ribbon or paper banding.

Twentieth Anniversary Cake

Theme: China

Inlay technique is used to decorate this unusual cake. The design is based on china created

by Clarice Cliff, whose 1930s Art Deco pieces became popular again in the 1970s.

Materials
20 x 25cm (8 x 10 inch)
oval cake
Apricot glaze
1kg (2lb) almond paste
1kg (2lb) candlelight
sugarpaste
Food colourings
250g (8oz) evergreen
sugarpaste
Clear alcohol (such as
vodka) for brushing
Icing sugar for dusting

Equipment
Two 25cm (10 inch)
round gâteau cards
Craft knife or scalpel
Pad of foam sponge
Scriber
Spacers
Sugarpaste smoother
5cm (2 inch) petunia
cutter (optional)
3cm (1¼ inch) leaf
cutter (optional)
5mm (¼ inch) plain
piping tube
Fine paintbrush
15 x 25cm (6 x 10 inch)
oblong cake board
(4mm/about ¼ inch
thick)

Preparation

1 Cut 5cm (2 inches) off one end of the cake and discard. This cut edge will become the base of the cake but it will be easier if most of the work is carried out with the cake lying flat.

2 Brush the cake with apricot glaze and cover the top and sides (but not the cut side) with the almond paste. Leave overnight.

3 Place the cake on a gâteau card and cut the card round the cake with a craft knife or scalpel. Fix the card to the cake with a little apricot glaze. Cut and fix a similar piece of gâteau card to the cut side of the cake (the base). (See Tips, page 24.)

4 Trace the design on page 47 on to greaseproof or non-stick paper, tracing only the main design for the lower part of the cake, omitting the smaller shape for the top. Don't worry about the outline of the cake at this stage. Mark the letters A and B on your tracing.

5 Colour 250g (8oz) candlelight sugarpaste orange, and a further 30g (1oz) violet. Work a little evergreen sugarpaste into another 30g (1oz) candlelight sugarpaste to create a pale green. Wrap all sugarpaste in plastic wrap until ready to use.

Covering the cake sides

6 Measure the depth of the sides of the cake. Place the traced design on the cake and mark a shallow indentation in the almond paste at the points marked A and B.

7 Roll out some evergreen sugarpaste and cut out two rectangles to fit the sides between point A and the base and point B and the base. Brush the almond paste with alcohol and fix the sugarpaste in position.

8 Measure the length of the remainder of the sides. Roll out some more candlelight sugarpaste and cut two strips, each long enough to fit round the remaining sides, and measuring one-third the depth of the cake. Use a ruler as a guide to obtain straight edges. Cut a similar strip from orange sugarpaste.

Tips

Fixing gâteau card to the 'back' of the cake saves on decorating and makes portioning the cake for serving easier – it can be taken off the board and laid down for cutting in the usual way. However, if the back of the cake is going to be seen, then it can be covered with plain sugarpaste, or the inlaid pattern repeated.

Covering the base of the cake with gâteau card serves two purposes – it prevents the cake from drying out whilst work on the decoration is in progress, and it creates a seal between the cake and the sugarpaste on the board when final assembly takes place.

9 Brush the almond paste on the sides of the cake with a little alcohol, and fix the sugarpaste strips to the sides, alternating the colours. Take care not to allow the strips to lose their shape. Leave overnight to dry.

10 Place the traced design on the cake, aligning points A and B with the joins in the evergreen and candlelight sugarpaste on the sides. Carefully mark the outline of the cake on to your tracing, following the outside edge of the sugarpaste on the sides of the cake.

11 Using the outline on page 47, add the small design for the top of the cake to your tracing.

Making the embosser

12 Place the tracing on a pad of foam sponge and, using the point of the scriber (or some other pointed implement), punch holes through the paper at intervals of about 5mm (¼ inch) all around the outlines of the design. The small round shapes on the right need only be marked at the centre point.

Inlaying the pattern

13 The use of spacers when rolling out will help achieve a consistent thickness of sugarpaste, which is essential.

14 Roll out the remaining candle-light sugarpaste on a thin board lightly dusted with icing sugar. Place the perforated tracing on top of the sugarpaste and gently rub over it with a sugarpaste smoother to transfer the punched markings to the paste. Remove the paper and cut straight across the sugarpaste from point A to point B, discarding the bottom portion.

15 Using petunia and leaf cutters, or carefully cutting with a knife along the perforation marks, cut the flower and leaf shapes out of the bottom edge of the sugarpaste. Use the tip of a piping tube as a small cutter for the motifs on the right of the picture. Cut out the top design with a knife. Cover with plastic wrap.

16 Roll out some evergreen and pale green sugarpaste. Cut out leaf shapes from each, and cut each in half lengthways. Fit the pieces together into the appropriate areas in the sugarpaste background. Roll out some violet, orange and more pale green sugarpaste and cut out flowers. Fit them carefully into position in the cut-out sugarpaste. Cut out a violet shape for the top decoration and fit it in carefully.

17 Roll out some more evergreen sugarpaste to the same thickness. Place the perforated design over it and emboss the sugarpaste with the perforations as before. Cut across between points A and B, cutting around the petal and leaf shapes, following the top of the evergreen area. Position the piece of

evergreen sugarpaste so that it butts up against the bottom of the main design. Using the icing smoother, polish all over the sugarpaste.

18 Place the perforated tracing face-down on the sugarpaste (so the indentations will not mark the surface), and cut round the outline.

19 Brush the almond paste on top of the cake with alcohol. Take the inlay design to the cake and carefully slide it off the board into position on top of the cake. Smooth into place and gently work in the edges. Leave overnight.

20 Using black food colouring and a fine paintbrush, paint in the small flower stems and centres.

Finishing
21 Cover the oblong cake board with candlelight sugarpaste. Moisten the centre of the board with cooled boiled water, then stand the cake upright on the board.

Twenty-fifth Anniversary Cake

Theme: Silver

Modern techniques are used for this pretty cake, though the silver favours

are a reminder of the type of wedding trimmings that were popular in the 1970s.

Materials

20 x 25cm (8 x 10 inch)
oblong cake
Apricot glaze
1kg (2lb) almond paste
Clear alcohol (such as
vodka) for brushing
1kg (2lb) white
sugarpaste
250g (8oz) royal icing
125g (4oz) modelling
paste (see page 41)
Silver food colouring
(see Note on page 29)
Silver dragees

Preparing the cake

1 Brush the cake with apricot glaze and cover with the almond paste. Brush the almond paste with alcohol and cover with the white sugarpaste. Reserve the trimmings. Centre the cake on the cake board and coat the board around the base of the cake with about half of the royal icing. Leave to dry.

2 Trace the template patterns on page 46 on to a folded double piece of greaseproof or non-stick paper, lining up the dotted fold lines on the outlines with the fold in the paper. Cut out the outlines round the solid lines and open them out to make two templates.

3 Fix the appropriate template to each side of the cake with masking tape. Using a scriber, mark guidelines along the tops of the templates on the sides of the cake. Remove the templates.

4 Using a paper piping bag fitted with a no. 3 piping tube, pipe a plain shell border in royal icing round the base of the cake.

Making the frills

5 Roll out some modelling paste thinly and cut out narrow rings with a scalloped frill cutter. Cover with plastic wrap. Frill one ring at a time by rolling the outside edges with a frilling tool or cocktail stick.

6 Brush along the scribed guidelines on the sides of the cake with a paintbrush moistened with a little water. Cut the frilled rings into strips and fix them along the guidelines, pressing gently to secure. Attach the second layer of frills 5mm (¼ inch) above the first. If wished, you can add a fine indented pattern by carefully running a tracing wheel along the second row of frills, just below the edge. Take care not to press too hard.

Equipment

33cm (13 inch) square
cake board
Masking tape
Scriber
Paper piping bags
Plain piping tubes (nos.
1, 2 and 3)
Garrett frill cutter
Frilling tool or cocktail
stick
Paintbrush
Tracing wheel (optional)
Waxed paper or
cellophane
Daisy cutters
Scalpel
Thin palette knife
8 silver horseshoes
5 double loops and tails
of 2.5mm (⅛ inch) white
ribbon (see page 17)

7 Finish the top edge of the frills with a piped scallop line, using a no. 1 tube and royal icing.

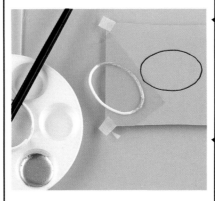

Making the plaques

8 Trace the oval plaque on page 46 on to greaseproof or non-stick paper, and make two copies on thicker paper. Cover each with a square of waxed paper or cellophane, and pipe the outlines on to the paper

or cellophane, using a no. 2 tube and royal icing. Allow to dry. Paint the ovals silver and leave to dry.

9 Flood the centres of the plaques with royal icing and leave to dry. The numerals are piped on to the plaques using royal icing and a no. 1 tube. When dry, the numbers can be finished off with silver food colouring.

The daisies

10 To make the daisies, roll out some modelling paste very thinly (see page 8), and cut out about 30 daisy shapes. Keep the flowers covered with plastic wrap while you work on one at a time.

11 Cut each daisy petal in half lengthways with a scalpel and roll each half on a board with the point of a frilling tool or cocktail stick. Lift each flower on a thin palette knife and place to set on crumpled foil (or in the plastic tray from a box of sweets). Leaving the flowers to dry on a crumpled surface will give them a more natural look.

Finishing

12 Fix the plaques to the centre of the front and back of the cake with a little royal icing. Place the horseshoes in pairs at each corner, fixing with a little more royal icing.

13 Mould a rounded oval of sugar-paste as a base for the daisies, moisten the underside with cooled boiled water or alcohol, and position in the centre of the top of the cake.

14 Arrange daisies over the mound, using the photograph on page 27 as a guide, and fixing them in position with a little royal icing (use a paper piping bag and a no. 2 tube). Place a silver dragee on a small dot of royal icing in the centre of each flower. Push the ribbon loops into the sugarpaste mound between the flowers, using a pair of tweezers.

15 Pipe a small bulb of royal icing at the foot of each pair of horse-shoes and place a daisy in position. Fix ribbon or paper banding round the board edge, if wished.

Note Whilst it is non-toxic, silver food colouring is not edible. Ensure the plaques are removed before the cake is cut.

Variations

The same design can be used for a golden wedding. Cover the cake with ivory or candlelight sugarpaste, and colour the lower frill a deep golden-yellow. Make daisies or roses from golden-yellow paste. The plaques may be replaced by piped or run-out monograms. Alternatively, position the flowers off-centre on the top of the cake, and add a monogram to balance the design.

Thirtieth Anniversary Cake

Theme: Pearl

The string of pearls at the base of this cake is easily removed before serving;

the remaining pearls on the cake are edible.

Materials

20x15cm (8x6 inch)
scalloped oval cake
Apricot glaze
750g (1½lb) almond
paste
Clear alcohol (such as
vodka) for brushing
1kg (2lb) tickled pink
sugarpaste
125g (4oz) pastillage
(see page 41)
Cornflour for dusting
Pink and silver glitter
powder food colouring
About 1 metre (1¼
yards) 'pearl string'
125g (4oz) pale pink
royal icing

1 Preparing the cake

Brush the cake with apricot glaze and cover with the almond paste. Brush the almond paste with alcohol and cover with the pink sugarpaste, reserving the excess. Using no. 2 crimpers, immediately crimp the pattern of squares (see page 33) on the back and front sides, and emboss the shell pattern on the two ends with the modelling tool. Leave to dry.

2

Roll out the spare sugarpaste and use to cover the cake board, trimming the edges cleanly. Centre the tin the cake was baked in, or a template of its base, on the coated board and cut the sugarpaste round the cake shape. Remove the centre section. Emboss the shell design round the edge of the board with the modelling tool.

3 Making the shells

Knead a walnut-sized ball of pastillage until smooth. Dust the surface lightly with cornflour and press it into a shell mould. Use your thumb to indent a hollow in the shell. Trim the excess pastillage from the shell, working from the centre towards the edges with a thin-bladed palette knife. Turn the shell out and leave to dry. Repeat to make the second shell (plus some spares in case one gets damaged). When dry, brush the shells inside and out with a mixture of pink and silver glitter powder food colouring. Set aside.

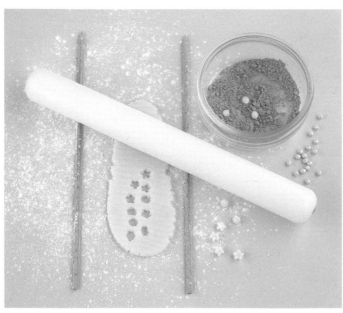

Equipment

Almond paste crimpers
(no. 2, open scallop)
Shell/blade modelling
tool
30x25cm (12x10 inch)
oval cake board
Shell mould
Thin-bladed palette
knife
Paintbrush
Spacers
Small blossom plunger
cutter
Piping bags
Plain piping tubes
(nos. 1 and 2)
Scriber
Pieces of foam sponge

The 'pearls'

4 Shape leftover almond paste or sugarpaste into tiny balls to make the edible 'pearls'. To achieve a uniform size, roll the paste thinly and evenly, using spacers to help achieve an equal thickness, and use a tiny cutter, such as a small blossom plunger cutter, to cut out the required number of pieces. (Make a few extra in case some get spoiled.) Roll each piece into a ball and leave on one side to crust over. Make 'pearls' in two different sizes – some for the sides and board, and some larger ones for the top ornament.

5 When the balls of paste are firm, roll them in a mixture of pink and silver glitter powder food colouring to give them a characteristic pearl sheen.

Finishing

6 Centre the cake on the coated board. Cut a length of 'pearl string' to fit around the base of the cake. Using royal icing and a no. 2 piping tube, pipe a line around the cake base and press the 'pearl string' into this to secure it, ensuring the join is at the back of the cake. Fix small sugarpaste or almond paste 'pearls' on the cake sides and on the board using dots of royal icing.

7 Trace the numerals on pages 4 and 5 on to greaseproof or non-stick paper, and scribe the outlines on to the cake top. Pipe over the outlines using a no. 1 tube and royal icing. Secure one half-shell on the cake top with a small bulb of royal icing. Arrange larger edible 'pearls' in the shell and on the cake top. Fix the second half-shell with bulbs of royal icing piped along the hinge edge of the shell. Prop the upper shell open with small pieces of foam sponge until the royal icing at the join is completely dry. Trim the board with ribbon or paper banding.

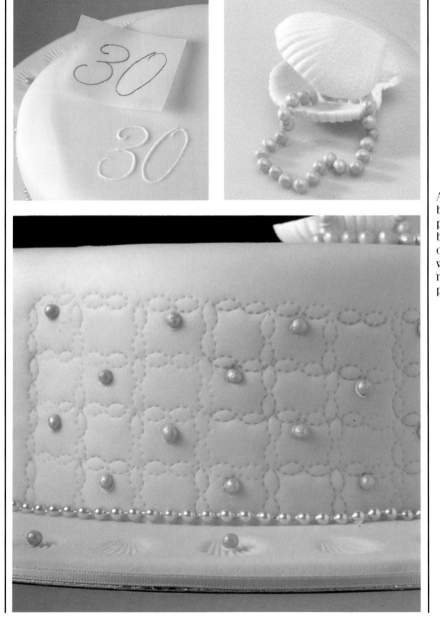

Tip
After coating the cake board, removing the paste which would lie beneath the cake not only saves waste but will prevent an unsightly mess when the cake is portioned for serving.

Fortieth Anniversary Cake

Theme: Ruby

Rejoicing lovebirds and elegant piping work set the scene for a celebration

of 40 years of marriage.

Materials
20cm (8 inch) round cake
Apricot glaze
1kg (2lb) almond paste
875g (1¾lb) royal icing
Ruby and brown food colourings

Equipment
28cm (11 inch) round cake board
Shaped icing scraper (see Tip on page 36)
Masking tape
Small paper piping bags
Waxed paper or cellophane
Angle-poise or desk lamp
Ribbon piping tube (no. 32R)
Plain piping tubes (nos. 1, 2 and 3)

1 **Preparing the cake**
Brush the cake with apricot glaze and cover with the almond paste. Place the cake on the board.

2 Coat the top and sides of the cake with two coats of royal icing tinted pale pink with ruby colouring, leaving each coat to dry for 24 hours. Cover the top of the cake and the sides with a third and final coat, using a shaped scraper to smooth the icing on the sides while it is still soft. Coat the board around the base of the cake with royal icing.

3 **Runout birds and bells**
Trace the design on page 46 on to greaseproof or non-stick paper, re-trace on to thicker paper, and fix to a flat surface with masking tape. The design is easier to work on if cut into three separate motifs. If necessary, make an extra tracing.

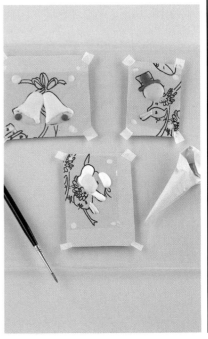

If you haven't got an icing scraper shaped like the one shown, make one from a piece of rigid plastic. Cut out the required shape with a hole-puncher.

4 Spoon small amounts of fresh royal icing into four bowls and colour separately in three tints of ruby and one of brown. Thin the icing, if necessary, to a consistency slightly softer than soft peak with a little water. Pour the icing into four separate paper piping bags and snip off the tips to roughly the size of a no. 2 piping tube.

5 Secure a piece of waxed paper or cellophane over each motif with dots of icing. Pipe each section of runout in the order shown on page 46. As soon as one stage of piping is complete, place the runouts under a hot angled lamp to crust over before going on to the next stage. If the icing is of the correct consistency it should

hold its shape without outlines. For the wings (stage 5), colour a separate batch of icing that is of normal piping consistency. Finally, leave the motifs to dry completely.

6 When the runouts are dry, remove them from the paper and fix them to the top of the cake with dots of royal icing. Using deep ruby royal icing and a no. 32R (ribbon) piping tube, pipe ribbon bows at the top of the bells, and ribbon tails for the birds to swing from.

7 Using a no. 1 tube and white royal icing, pipe eyeballs on the birds. With brown royal icing and a no. 1 tube, pipe beaks, feet and pupils. With deep ruby royal icing and a no. 1 tube, add a ribbon and bow to the female's hat, and a bow tie to the male bird's neck.

Piping the borders

8 Using a no. 3 tube and pale ruby royal icing, pipe bulbs around the top edge of the cake. Change to a bag fitted with a no. 1 tube and pipe dropped loops from the bulbs. Starting in the centre of one bulb, drop the loop, miss two bulbs and connect the icing again to the third bulb along. Break off and go back to the first missed bulb, attach the icing and repeat the process all round the cake. Pipe a second row of loops from the joins in the first row.

9 Pipe similar large bulbs all around the base of the cake, and pipe loops above them from the shaped flange on the cake side.

Finishing

10 Pipe a tiny heart in the centre of each bulb on the top border, using a no. 1 tube and pale ruby royal icing. Change to a bag fitted with a no. 2 tube and pipe a scalloped line on the cake top, following the shape of the bulb border.

11 With a piping bag fitted with a no. 1 tube and filled with medium ruby royal icing, pipe a dot at each join in the scalloped piping on the cake top. Pipe another scalloped line above the flange on the cake side, and tiny hearts on the cake board, between each bulb.

12 Trim the cake board with ribbon or paper banding.

Fiftieth Anniversary Cake

Theme: Gold

These faithful companions in the fish tank are sure to raise a smile

for a couple marking their fiftieth anniversary.

Materials
20cm (8 inch) square
cake
Apricot glaze
1kg (2lb) almond paste
875g (1¾lb) royal icing
Food colourings
125g (4oz) evergreen
sugarpaste
Clear alcohol (such as
vodka) for brushing
Golden-yellow powder
food colouring
(optional)
Asparagus fern

Equipment
28cm (11 inch) square
cake board
Palette knife
Icing scraper
Paintbrush
Masking tape
Paper piping bags
Angle-poise or desk
lamp
Airbrush (optional)
Plain piping tubes (nos.
1 and 2)
Scriber
Gold coloured '50'
favour (optional)

Preparing the cake

1 Brush the cake with apricot glaze and cover with almond paste. Place on the cake board.

2 Coat the top and sides of the cake with two coats of blue-green royal icing, leaving each coat to dry for 24 hours. Coat the top in a third coat of the same colour.

3 For the final coat on the sides, colour batches of the royal icing in deeper shades of blue-green. Paddle this round the sides with a palette knife, using the deepest shade at the base and graduating to the palest at the top. Smooth with an icing scraper. Coat the cake board around the base of the cake in the deepest shade of blue-green icing.

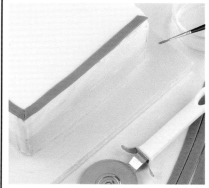

Making the 'tank'

4 Measure the sides and depth of the cake. Roll out the evergreen sugarpaste and cut strips to form edges at the top and corners. Brush the backs of the strips with alcohol to secure the sugarpaste to the royal icing on the cake.

Making the fish

5 Trace the fish on page 47 on to greaseproof or non-stick paper, re-trace on to thicker paper, and fix to a flat surface with masking tape. Cut pieces of waxed paper or cellophane a little larger than the motifs and place over the drawings, securing with three or four dots of royal icing.

6 Colour some full peak royal icing pale golden-yellow, and thin to a consistency slightly softer than soft peak. Pour into a small paper piping bag and snip off the tip to roughly the size of a no. 2 tube. Pipe the icing to cover the fish designs, piping the fins and tails first before filling in the bodies.

7 When each fish has been piped, slide a palette knife under the paper and move it to a flat board. Leave under a hot lamp to dry, then colour the backs by spraying with an airbrush or brushing with dry powder colour in golden-yellow. Pipe features (eyes and mouths) using royal icing and a piping bag fitted with a plain no. 1 tube.

Finishing
8 Trace the inscription on page 47 and scribe on to the top of the cake. Pipe, using a no. 1 tube and deep blue-green royal icing.

9 Secure the goldfish to the cake sides with dots of royal icing. Using white royal icing of soft peak consistency, and a no. 2 tube, pipe 'bubbles' on cake sides and top.

10 Mix assorted colours of royal icing – grey, green, blue, pink – and put into small piping bags. Cut the ends to roughly the size of a no. 3 tube and pipe rough gravel shapes at the base of the cake.

11 Cut short pieces of asparagus fern and push into piped 'gravel' to secure. Fix the '50' favour in place with a few dots of royal icing (optional). Trim the board edge with ribbon or paper band.

Basic Recipes

This section contains recipes for specific pastes and icings

required for some of the cake designs, plus a delicious buttercream recipe and

some lighter alternatives to traditional rich fruit cake.

Modelling Paste

This paste has been used throughout the book for drapes, frills and flowers. You may have a favourite petal paste recipe to use for flowers but, if not, this is an easy paste to make and is quite adequate for unwired flowers. It will keep at room temperature for several weeks.

Makes 250g (8oz)
1 teaspoon gum tragacanth or 30g (1oz) bought petal paste
250g (8oz) sugarpaste

Work the two ingredients together until you have a smooth paste. Wrap in a double layer of plastic wrap and store at room temperature.

Pastillage

This is a very hard-setting pastillage which is useful for ornaments and plaque-making.

500g (1lb/3 cups) icing sugar
3 tablespoons cornflour
2 teaspoons powdered gelatine
60ml (2fl oz/¼ cup) cold water
30g (1oz) royal icing

1 Sift together the icing sugar and cornflour and put it in a heatproof bowl. Place over a saucepan of hot but not boiling water and heat to 70°C (150°F).

2 Sprinkle the gelatine over the cold water in a small heatproof bowl. Leave to soften for 2–3 minutes. Stand the bowl over a saucepan of hot but not boiling water, and stir gently until the gelatine has completely dissolved.

3 Add the dissolved gelatine to the dry ingredients and mix to a smooth, dry paste. Work in the royal icing and knead well. Double-wrap tightly in plastic wrap and store in a covered container.

Royal Icing for Runouts

The icing used for runouts requires stronger albumen than regular royal icing. The basic recipe given here may be adjusted to the correct consistency by thinning the icing with a little water. *The times given are approximate since mixer speeds differ.*

Makes about 1.75kg (3½lb)

60g (2oz/¼ cup) powdered albumen
315ml (10fl oz/1¼ cups) water
1.75kg (3½lb/10½ cups) icing sugar

1 Reconstitute the albumen in the water in a grease-free bowl. Add three-quarters of the icing sugar and beat with an electric mixer for about 2 minutes on slow speed.

2 Adjust the consistency with the remaining sugar and beat for about 3 minutes more on slow speed until the icing peaks.

Variation

To make a small quantity of runout icing by hand, reconstitute 4 teaspoons powdered albumen in 7 teaspoons water, and beat in 220g (7oz/1¼ cups) icing sugar.

Madeira Cake

Rich fruit cake is still the favoured base for British celebration cakes but occasionally something lighter may be called for. This Madeira cake can be split and layered with jam and/or a filling cream (such as the Fondant Buttercream on page 43), and may be covered with almond paste and icing in exactly the same way as a fruit cake. It freezes well, undecorated, and will keep for several days after cutting. The glycerine added to the recipe helps to keep the cake moist; the vegetable fat aids aeration; and the use of a special 'sponge' flour now available makes for a finer texture.

Two sets of ingredients are listed so this recipe can be adapted for all the cakes in this book. Make up the smaller quantity for the First (Cotton), Seventh (Copper), Thirteenth (Lace), Thirtieth (Pearl) and Fortieth (Ruby) anniversary cakes. For the remaining cakes, make up the larger quantity.

large cake

315g (10oz/2½ cups) sponge flour
125g (4oz/1 cup) plain (all-purpose) flour
315g (10oz) butter, softened
60g (2oz) white vegetable fat (shortening)
375g (12oz/1½ cups) caster (superfine) sugar
3 teaspoons glycerine
7 eggs (size 2), beaten
grated rind and juice of 1½ lemons or oranges

small cake

220g (7oz/1¾ cups) sponge flour
90g (3oz/¾ cup) plain (all-purpose) flour
220g (7oz) butter, softened
30g (1oz) white vegetable fat (shortening)
250g (8oz/1¼ cups) caster (superfine) sugar
2 teaspoons glycerine
5 large eggs (size 2), beaten
grated rind and juice of 1 lemon or orange

1 Make sure all the ingredients are at room temperature. Preheat the oven to 190°C (375°F/Gas 5). Grease the required tin and line with greaseproof or non-stick paper. Sift the sponge and plain flours together.

2 Cream the butter, white fat and sugar together in a bowl until pale and fluffy. Beat in the glycerine, then add the eggs, a little at a time, together with a spoonful of flour, beating well after each addition.

3 Fold the remaining flour into the creamed mixture together with the lemon or orange rind and juice. Turn into the prepared tin and level the surface.

4 Place the cake in the centre of the oven and immediately reduce the oven heat to 160°C (325°F/Gas 3). Bake for about 1 hour 20 minutes or until well risen, firm to the touch and golden brown in colour.

5 Stand the tin on a wire cooling rack for 20–30 minutes before turning out the cake and leaving to cool completely.

Light Fruit Cake

This Genoa cake is a popular alternative to heavily fruited cakes, especially with young people. Two sets of ingredients are given so this recipe can be adapted for all the cakes in this book. Make up the smaller quantity for the First (Cotton), Seventh (Copper), Thirteenth (Lace), Thirtieth (Pearl) and Fortieth (Ruby) anniversary cakes. For the remaining cakes, make up the larger quantity.

large cake

220g (7oz/1¼ cups) sultanas
(golden raisins)
310g (10oz/2 cups) currants
60g (2oz/⅓ cup) chopped
mixed peel
235g (7½oz/scant 1½ cups) glacé
cherries, diced
90g (3oz) glycerine
185g (6oz) butter, softened
45g (1½oz) white vegetable fat
(shortening)
235g (7½oz/generous 1 cup)
caster (superfine) sugar
5 large eggs (size 2), beaten
45g (1½oz/⅓ cup) self-raising
flour
310g (10oz/2½ cups) plain
(all-purpose) flour
20g (¾oz) ground almonds

small cake

155g (5oz/1 cup) sultanas
220g (7oz/1½ cups) currants
45g (1½oz/¼ cup) chopped
mixed peel
155g (5oz/1 cup) glacé
cherries, diced
60g (2oz) glycerine
125g (4oz) butter, softened
30g (1oz) white vegetable fat
(shortening)
155g (5oz/⅔ cup) caster
(superfine) sugar
3 large eggs (size 1), beaten
30g (1oz/¼ cup) self-raising flour
220g (7oz/1¾ cups) plain
(all-purpose) flour
15g (½oz) ground almonds

1 Mix the sultanas, currants, peel and glacé cherries together in a large bowl. Pour the glycerine over, cover and leave to stand overnight.

2 Make sure all the ingredients are at room temperature. Preheat the oven to 200°C (400°F/Gas 6). Grease the required tin and line with greaseproof or non-stick paper. Sift the self-raising and plain flours together.

3 Cream the butter, white fat and sugar together in a bowl until pale and fluffy. Add the eggs, a little at a time, together with a spoonful of flour, beating well after each addition. Add the ground almonds and mix through. Fold in the mixed fruit and remaining flour. Turn into the prepared tin and level the surface.

4 Place the cake in the centre of the oven and immediately reduce the oven heat to 180°C (350°F/Gas 4). Bake for about 1½ hours or until well risen, firm to the touch and golden brown in colour.

5 Stand the tin on a wire cooling rack for about 1 hour before turning out the cake and leaving to cool completely.

Fondant Buttercream

This superior version of buttercream is wonderfully smooth and mellow. It is made using confectioners' (boiled) fondant in place of icing sugar. Many specialist cake-decorating shops now sell ready-made boiled fondant, but you may have a favourite recipe of your own that you prefer to use. It is important to use unsalted butter to make this buttercream so that added flavourings are not spoiled.

Makes about 500g (1lb)

280g (9oz) ready-made boiled
(continental) fondant
250g (8oz) unsalted butter,
softened

1 Soften the fondant by working pieces of it between your fingers until it is smooth.

2 Cream the butter in a bowl, then add the fondant, a little at a time, until it is all incorporated. Beat until smooth.

3 Colourings and flavourings (e.g. orange juice or orange liqueur) may be added to taste.

Thirteenth Anniversary Cake
(page 18)

side template

Seventh Anniversary Cake
(page 10)

collar template

On our First Anniversary

Fortieth Anniversary Cake
(page 34)

Twenty-fifth Anniversary Cake
(page 26)

plaque

short side

long side

Twentieth Anniversary Cake
(page 22)

Acknowledgements

The author would like to thank the following for their assistance:

Gordano Packaging Ltd
Unit 2a, Lansdowne Industrial Estate,
Cheltenham,
Gloucester GL51 8PL

Sefcol (Sales) Ltd
Whitehouse Industrial Estate,
Runcorn,
Cheshire WA7 3BJ
who supplied the sugarpaste and
almond paste

Mike Williams,
Head of Bakery Section,
Cornwall College,
Pool,
Redruth,
Cornwall TR15 3RD

The Publisher would like to thank the following suppliers:

**Anniversary House
(Cake Decorations) Ltd**
Unit 16,
Elliott Road,
West Howe Industrial Estate,
Bournemouth, BH11 8LZ

Cake Art Ltd
Venture Way,
Crown Estate,
Priorswood,
Taunton, TA2 8DE

Guy, Paul and Co. Ltd
Unit B4,
Foundry Way,
Little End Road,
Eaton Socon,
Cambs., PE19 3JH

Squires Kitchen
Squires House,
3 Waverley Lane,
Farnham,
Surrey, GU9 8BB